3 1994 00836 6020

[AUG   1996]

SANTA ANA PUBLIC LIBRARY
MCFADDEN BRANCH

D1505723

CHAMPLAIN
A LIFE OF COURAGE

CHAMPLAIN
A LIFE OF COURAGE

by William Jay Jacobs

B CHAMPLAIN,S.

J ~~971.0113~~ JAC
Jacobs, William Jay
Champlain

$19.90
31994008366020

MCFADDEN

Franklin Watts
New York / Chicago / London / Toronto / Sydney
A First Book

Cover illustration by Amy Wasserman
Cover map copyright © North Wind Picture Archives, Alfred, Me.
Cover photograph copyright © Stock Montage/Historical Pictures Service, Chicago, Il.

Photographs copyright ©: The Public Archives of Canada: p. 2; North Wind Picture
Archives: pp. 8, 12, 14, 21, 23, 24, 26, 27, 28, 31, 34, 35, 38, 40, 41, 47, 48, 51, 53;
The Bettmann Archive: p. 15; Art Resource Inc.: pp. 18 (Giraudon), 20, 56 (both
Lauros-Giraudon); Fort Ticonderoga Museum: p. 37; Nova Scotia Information
Service: p. 43; Stock Montage/Historical Pictures Service: p. 45

Library of Congress Cataloging-in-Publication Data

Jacobs, William Jay.
Champlain: a life of courage / by William Jay Jacobs.
p. cm. — (A First book)
Includes bibliographical references (p.) and index.
ISBN 0-531-20112-0
1. Champlain, Samuel de, 1567–1635—Juvenile literature.
2. Explorers—America—Biography—Juvenile literature.
3. Explorers—France—Biography—Juvenile literature.
4. New France—Discovery and exploration—French—Juvenile literature.
5. America—Discovery and exploration—French—Juvenile literature.
6. New France—Discovery and exploration. [1. Champlain,
Samuel de, 1567–1635. 2. Explorers.] I. Title. II. Series. F1030.1.J315 1994
971.01'13'092—dc20   93-31176
[B]   CIP AC

Copyright © 1994 by William Jay Jacobs
All rights reserved
Printed in the United States of America
6 5 4 3 2

CONTENTS

Not of the sunlight,
Not of the moonlight,
Not of the starlight!
O young Mariner,
Down to the haven,
Call your companions,
Launch your vessel
And crowd your canvas,
And, ere it vanishes
Over the margin,
After it, follow it,
Follow the Gleam.

—ALFRED LORD TENNYSON

PREFACE
A
LIFE
OF
COURAGE

Samuel de Champlain is known to history as "the Father of New France." It was Champlain who risked his life to find new paths to the Canadian interior. It was Champlain who mapped the eastern coastline of North America from the Saint Lawrence River to Cape Cod and prepared the first charts of Atlantic Ocean coast harbors as far south as present-day Boston. In addition to exploring the land destined to become France's empire in North America, he wrote four books about this vast, wild continent and its people.

It was Champlain who first understood that the real wealth of Canada was not in gold but rather in furs, fish, timber, and farmland.

For more than thirty years, Champlain worked to spread the Catholic religion among the Indians.

Finally, it was Champlain who founded the magnificent city of Quebec, and his personal strength and courage made that city's survival possible.

Courage and self-sacrifice are the main themes of

9

Champlain's life. However, his story also is one of thrilling adventure. He fought heroic battles against impossible odds. He dared to thrust a birchbark canoe into white-water rapids, feared even by skilled Indian warriors much younger than he was. He spent days and nights in the open air among people whose trust had to be won if New France were to survive.

Few men in the history of North America ever lived more exciting, more important lives than did Samuel de Champlain.

CHAPTER ONE

EARLY ADVENTURES

Like that of so many of history's great figures, little is known of the early life of Champlain. We do know that he was born in the town of Brouage, then a bustling seaport on the southwestern coast of France, some 70 miles (112 km) north of Bordeaux.

We do not know, however, whether he was born to a Protestant or a Catholic family, what he looked like as a youth, or how he was educated. Even the exact date of his birth is uncertain, although the year 1567 usually is accepted as an accurate guess.

As a young man, Champlain was caught up in the great Wars of Religion then sweeping across France. In 1586, the French Protestants (known as Huguenots) fought the Catholics for control of Brouage, and Champlain sided with the Catholics. The bitter religious wars dragged on until 1598, when King Henry IV, who had converted to Catholicism in 1593, finally won a complete victory.

Champlain had fought on land and sea in those

*After years of bitter conflict and struggle with
neighboring nations, King Henry IV finally won
a complete victory in the Wars of Religion in 1593.*

great struggles. He had seen men die, often needlessly, for their beliefs. From his years as a warrior he also had learned much. Probably thirty-one years old when peace came, he knew how to live in the open and how to take care of himself in freezing temperatures, sometimes without shelter. He knew how to survive with little to eat or to drink. He knew how to use tricks of ambush and surprise in skirmishes between small units of men. Those skills would serve him well in the wilderness of North America.

With the end of the Wars of Religion, Champlain was a soldier without a job. Yet he did not remain idle for long. Making his way to the coast of Brittany, he convinced his uncle, a ship's master working for the Spaniards there, to find a place for him on the *Saint Julien,* a vessel bound for Cádiz, Spain.

In Spain, the *Saint Julien* was chosen to sail with other ships to visit Spanish outposts in the New World. Champlain somehow won permission to go along. It was just the chance he had hoped for.

By early spring of 1598, the Spanish fleet had crossed the Atlantic Ocean. The ships threaded their way among the Virgin Islands, finally casting anchor in the magnificent harbor of what today is San Juan, Puerto Rico.

Champlain, an artist as well as a soldier, recorded his travels in a series of notes and colorful drawings. He sketched the trees and plants, as well as the animals,

Galleons such as these carried conquistadores and explorers from Spain to the Americas in search of gold, trading opportunities, and converts to Catholicism.

birds, and fish. He took special care in portraying the dark-skinned people who sometimes fled at the sight of the Spaniards.

After leaving Puerto Rico, Champlain visited Mexico. There he was amazed at the beauty of the countryside, and the wealth of Mexico City, with its temples, palaces, and houses still superb despite the great damage caused by Hernando Cortés and his conquering Spanish army.

But it was the plight of the Indians of Mexico that moved Champlain most deeply. Beaten, tortured, and

Hernando Cortés and his army conquering and destroying the ancient Aztec civilization.

enslaved by the Spaniards, the Indians were forced to declare themselves Catholics. If they refused to do so, they were burned to death.

Champlain watched carefully. He saw that the Indians never could be forced to believe in the white man's God. To him, it seemed they could be led to this faith only through kindness. That lesson was stored in his mind for the future.

Before starting back for Spain, the *Saint Julien* stopped at other Spanish possessions. Champlain noted the advantages of digging a canal there at the narrow Isthmus of Panama, the very location of the future Panama Canal.

Champlain and his companions returned to Spain two years and eight months after leaving. They had not lost a single ship in their voyage.

CHAPTER TWO
FIRST VOYAGE
TO
CANADA

On his return to France, Champlain gave King Henry IV a detailed report of his travels, complete with maps and watercolor illustrations. The king granted Champlain a small yearly income in payment for his past service in the Wars of Religion and a title of nobility in appreciation of his recent service in the Americas. Ever afterward, the explorer would be permitted to sign his name Samuel *de* Champlain, the *de* marking him as a man of noble rank.

King Henry was eager to learn more about the Americas. He thought that if Frenchmen were to live there, they someday might send great wealth back to France, just as Spanish colonists had to Spain. The king therefore arranged for Champlain to visit Canada along with a party commanded by François Gravé (usually known as "Pontgravé"). When Champlain and the good-natured Pontgravé first met they immediately liked each other. Their friendship was destined to last a lifetime.

King Henry IV granted Champlain a title of nobility and a yearly income, and arranged for him to travel to Canada in search of wealth and territory for France.

The expedition, consisting of three ships, left France on March 15, 1603. Less than two months later, on May 7, the Frenchmen sighted the coast of Newfoundland. For Champlain it was to be the first of eleven trips across the Atlantic Ocean to Canada.

What was it about this strange new land, Canada, that so fascinated the French? Francis Parkman, one of America's greatest historians, painted a word picture of it in his book, *Pioneers of France in the New World*. To him, Canada was "an untamed continent; vast wastes of

18

forest…mountains silent in primeval sleep; river, lake, and glimmering pool; wilderness oceans mingling with the sky."

Long before the official French expedition, many Europeans had come to Canada. Medieval legends told of islands lying "beyond the setting sun." Portuguese explorers searching for those very islands may have reached America, perhaps twenty years before the voyage of Columbus in 1492. So had French fishermen who, almost certainly, dried their rich catches near the Grand Banks of Newfoundland. Long before that, hardy Norsemen, sailing from Iceland and Greenland in search of ship timber and supplies, had come upon the Canadian coast.

In 1497, John Cabot planted a cross and a British flag somewhere on the coast, probably in Newfoundland. Then, in 1524, Giovanni da Verrazano, an Italian sailing for France, landed perhaps as far north as Cape Breton.

But France's strongest claim to the North American continent came with the voyages of Jacques Cartier, a fisherman and explorer. Setting sail in 1534 with two ships and sixty men furnished by the French king, he raised a cross 30 feet high (9 m) at Canada's mighty Gaspé Peninsula. Cartier also visited Newfoundland and Labrador. On a later voyage, he sailed up the Saint Lawrence River to the location of present-day Montreal.

Trade steadily increased between the French and the Indians. Efforts to set up permanent French settle-

This Theodore Gudin painting from 1847
depicts Jacques Cartier and his party
discovering the St. Lawrence River.

ments in Canada were unsuccessful, however, and French profits from trading remained low.

It was to solve such problems that Champlain and Pontgravé first embarked on their voyage. On May 27, 1603, they landed at Tadoussac, on the Saint Lawrence River, the usual meeting place each summer of French fur traders and Indians.

We know little about Champlain's appearance at the

20

*Fur trading was a profitable
business for both the French
and the Indians in Canada.*

time. But from his own drawings and the work of some historians it is possible to imagine him. Probably he was of less than medium height, lean with dark hair and dark eyes. People spoke of him as tough and energetic. And, with the Indians, he seldom complained, even when he was in great pain. His comrades spoke of him as honest and sincere. They trusted him.

The Indians received Champlain and Pontgravé with great courtesy. Together, the Frenchmen and the Indians gathered in the lodge of an Algonquin Indian chief. There, for a long time, they sat in a circle, silently smoking tobacco in long pipes.

Slowly and carefully, the Indian chief began to speak. He called for French armies to help him make war against the hated, dreaded enemy of the Algonquin tribe: the Iroquois nation.

When the chief finished speaking, the Indians cried out together, "Ho, ho, ho!" which meant yes, yes, yes!

Champlain and Pontgravé agreed to help. True, they knew that the Iroquois probably were more powerful and later might ally with the British. However, they had little choice, for their interest was mostly in fur trading along the Saint Lawrence River, and the Algonquins controlled that river. Without the Indians' friendship the trade route would be blocked.

After completing their treaty of friendship with the Algonquins, the Frenchmen made their way farther up the Saint Lawrence River. Just before reaching the location of present-day Montreal, they were stopped by the powerful Lachine Rapids, which made it impossible for them to proceed except in canoes. They decided not to go on.

Before returning to Newfoundland, Champlain questioned the Algonquins in detail about a possible "great water" passageway across Canada, to the Pacific Ocean. Such a passageway would enable him to sail west to China and the East Indies lands of fabled riches. To Champlain, it would be a "Passage to India."

Neither he nor the explorers of any other nation then knew that such a passageway did not exist anywhere in North America. Until well into the 1700s, people continued to look for it, and as they did, they managed to explore the North American continent.

By the autumn of 1603, Champlain had seen rich farmlands in Canada. He returned to Newfoundland with valuable furs to load in the hold of his ship.

The Lachine Rapids in the St. Lawrence River were initially a barrier to Champlain's expedition into Canada.

*The frontiers of Canada held the
promise of great wealth for the French
settlers and for the monarchy in France.*

The return voyage across the Atlantic took only
eighteen days. To Champlain and his French comrades,
contact with the New World was beginning to appear
quite manageable. It would prove, however, to be far
more difficult than anyone then could imagine.

CHAPTER THREE

ACADIA

Champlain's report of his voyage greatly pleased King Henry IV of France, especially the exciting news that there might be a water route through Canada to China and the East Indies. The king gave permission for Champlain's report to be printed as a book, *Des Sauvages*, perhaps best translated *Natives*.

While Champlain's expedition was in North America, its sponsor had died. However, one of the king's close comrades, Pierre da Gua, Sieur de Monts, offered to help pay for the further exploration and settlement of Canada. In exchange, de Monts was to receive a monopoly of the fur trade for ten years. Champlain agreed to serve de Monts as mapmaker and geographer, without receiving any special rank or title.

De Monts quickly obtained money from the merchants of several French coastal towns for another voyage to Canada. In the spring of 1604, the expedition set sail with Pontgravé once again in official command.

DES SAVVAGES,

OV,

VOYAGE DE SAMVEL CHAMPLAIN, DE BROVAGE, fait en la France nouuelle, l'an mil six cens trois:

CONTENANT

Les mœurs, façon de viure, mariages, guerres, & habitations des Sauuages de Canadas.

De la descouuerte de plus de quatre cens cinquante lieuës dans le païs des Sauuages. Quels peuples y habitent, des animaux qui s'y trouuent, des riuieres, lacs, isles & terres, & quels arbres & fruicts elles produisent.

De la coste d'Arcadie, des terres que l'on y a descouuertes, & de plusieurs mines qui y sont, selon le rapport des Sauuages.

A PARIS,

Chez CLAVDE DE MONSTR'ŒIL, tenant sa boutique en la Cour du Palais, au nom de Iesus.

AVEC PRIVILEGE DV ROY

The title page from Champlain's book that reported the explorer's findings to King Henry IV.

Promised a ten-year fur trade monopoly, Pierre da Gua, Sieur de Monts, agreed to finance Champlain's 1604 expedition to Canada.

This time, de Monts recruited for the journey some 120 carpenters, masons, and soldiers. In Canada, he hoped to trade for furs and to explore the land. He also hoped to start a permanent French colony there.

France's claim to land in the New World was known as Acadia. It was made up of the territory between the Saint Lawrence River and the Atlantic Ocean, and included what are known today as Nova Scotia, New Brunswick, and eastern Maine.

De Monts chose Saint Croix Island, at today's boundary between Maine and Canada to be the center of the colony. Few choices could have been worse. The island had little fresh water. Its soil would support no crops. In wintertime, it was unprotected from fierce northwest winds.

In 1604, winter set in early, and with it came deep snows. Great blocks of ice floated on 25-foot (7.5 m) tides in the channel that separates the island from the coast.

Snowbound inside their huts, the Frenchmen were limited to a diet made up mostly of salted meats and dried fish. Many suffered from scurvy. Flesh hung in the mouths of the sick, their gums becoming so soft that their teeth fell out. The arms and legs of many men became swollen. Pain racked their stomachs. Many of them coughed and spat blood.

According to Champlain, of the seventy-nine men on Saint Croix Island that winter, thirty-five died and twenty others nearly died.

In June, relief ships arrived from France. De Monts, eager to find a milder climate for the colony, ordered Champlain to sail southward along the Atlantic coast-line with a small force.

From 1603 to 1615, Samuel de Champlain explored the coast and interior of Canada.

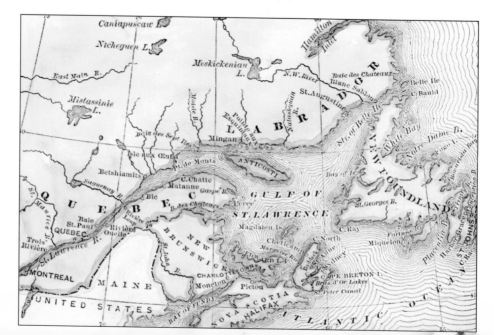

During the summer of 1605, Champlain and his party visited the locations of present-day Wiscasset, Portland, Old Orchard Beach, Biddeford, and Kennebunkport in what today is known as Maine. On July 16, 1605, they sailed up the Charles River past the location of present-day Boston. Almost certainly, Champlain and his shipmates were the very first white men ever to look on Boston Harbor.

From there, the French sailed south to the location of what now is the town of Plymouth, and proceeded along the shore of Cape Cod past the location of today's Provincetown. Indians often appeared on the sandy beaches to wave at them and to dance.

Probably, it was the sight of so many Indians that caused de Monts to turn northward and return to Saint Croix Island. He feared that a French colony might not survive among the Indians. In addition, Cape Cod had few fine furs, and it was furs that would return the greatest profits in the marketplaces of Europe.

This decision of de Monts proved crucial. If he had decided otherwise, a French colony might well have been planted as far south as the location of present-day Boston, or even that of New York City, instead of in Quebec. The history of the world might have been vastly different.

Instead, de Monts sent Champlain and Pontgravé to find a safe winter base on the sheltered western coast of Nova Scotia. The two men chose the beautiful, well-protected harbor of Port Royal, near Annapolis Royal, and it was there that they spent the winter of 1605–1606. They hunted, fished, and passed the dreary evenings around a blazing fire, singing, drinking wine, and telling stories.

De Monts, meanwhile, had returned to France for more soldiers. Few Frenchmen, however, were interested in becoming soldiers and serving in Canada. By the time he returned to Canada, winter was approaching. While waiting for his commander, Champlain had been able to explore perhaps only as far south and west as the channel that separates Martha's Vineyard from the mainland.

Without that delay, the Frenchmen probably would have reached the Connecticut shore and the mouth of the Hudson River at Manhattan. There they would have been received by friendly Indians of the region. Instead, the colder Canadian latitudes were to become the home of French colonists in the North America.

When the winter of 1606–1607 arrived, Champlain was well prepared. He organized hunting contests during the daytime and formal dinners and musical productions in the evenings. With his own high spirits, he worked to keep the French soldiers from boredom and fighting among themselves during the long winter indoors.

Also during that winter, Champlain came to know the Indians of Acadia, who were called Micmacs (or Sourquois). Micmac women and children enjoyed visit-

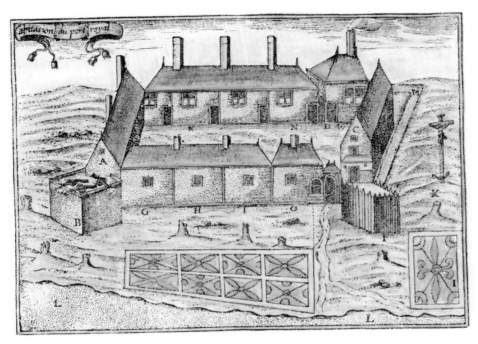

Above: *Champlain's drawing of his settlement*
Port Royal near Annapolis Royal
Below: *Micmacs from the area surrounding Acadia*
were regular guests at Port Royal.

ing the French encampment. Several of the Indian chiefs regularly ate with the Frenchmen. One of the chiefs later became a deeply religious Christian.

At this time, Champlain came to like the Indians. He respected their strength and courage, and he admired their ability to survive in the wilderness. He appreciated their arts especially the animals, birds, and fish they carved from stone and wood, as well as their music and their dances.

Most of all, he learned to know the Indians as people, each man and woman with a different personality, neither all good nor all bad. Thus, when Champlain finally gained his own command of French forces in Canada, he knew how to deal with the Indians, treating them simply as people, like himself. He kept his promises and expected them to do the same.

Unlike so many of the British, Dutch, and Spanish leaders, Champlain never looked down on the Indians, or treated them as members of an inferior race. Instead, he met them as equals: ate their food and lived his life with them. He set an example for other Frenchmen. And that is why the French and Indians stayed on such friendly terms.

Champlain believed that Europeans and Indians should live together in peace. For without peace, trade would be impossible, and no French colony in Canada ever could hope to survive and prosper. To Samuel de Champlain, it was the dream of a prosperous French empire in North America that mattered most.

32

CHAPTER FOUR

QUEBEC

In April 1608, Champlain and his companion Pontgravé sailed up the Saint Lawrence River to a place that both men knew well. It was the ideal location for a colony. There, properly placed cannons could control river traffic, and soaring cliffs could protect the settlers and the soldiers.

The place was Quebec. It was to be the earliest permanent city north of Mexico City and Florida to be settled by white men. July 3, 1608, was the date of its founding.

Through the rest of the summer, Champlain busied himself preparing for the coming winter weather. He called the building that housed his settlement the "Habitation" and designed many of its features himself.

Suddenly, the work of the colony came to a halt. A few of the French workers, angered by the hard work they had to do, hatched a plot. They planned to kill Champlain and sell the new fort to French traders at the trading post of Tadoussac. Then they would return to Europe as wealthy men.

Champlain discovered the plot. He captured the

Champlain designed and built the "Habitation," the first permanent housing constructed in Quebec.

conspirators and quickly arranged a trial. A jury, made up of officers and enlisted men, soon decided on the death penalty for the ringleader, Jean Duval.

Duval was strangled to death and then, as an example to others, his head was mounted on a pike at the highest point of the fortress. The three other plotters were sent back to France in chains.

This was one of the few times in all of Champlain's career that he dealt out justice harshly. Usually he was gentle and forgiving, especially in his handling of the Indians, even when their murder of a Frenchman was concerned.

Soon there were other problems to handle. By the spring of 1609, disease had taken a heavy toll in Quebec. Ten men died of scurvy, five of dysentery. Then the colony's doctor died. Even the hardy Champlain fell ill.

By June, when a relief ship arrived from France, only eight lonely white men, half of them sick, were able to greet it. Still, the settlement somehow managed to survive, and Champlain began taking steps to make his dream of a French empire in America a reality.

His plan was risky. Instead of staying safely in a fortified trading post (like Tadoussac) on the Saint Lawrence River, he hoped to open the wild interior of Canada, with all of its possible wealth, to French settlement.

To do that, he formed an alliance with the Huron and Algonquin Indians, even though he knew that the

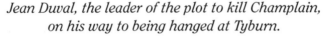

Jean Duval, the leader of the plot to kill Champlain,
on his way to being hanged at Tyburn.

price of such an alliance could be high. It almost certainly would mean war with the ancient enemy of those two tribes, the mighty Iroquois.

On July 30, 1609, war did break out. Its first battle probably was fought near the location of the future Fort Ticonderoga, so important nearly two hundred years later during the American Revolution.

According to Champlain's own account, the Hurons and the Algonquins lined up face-to-face with the hated Iroquois. Before the fighting began, however, Champlain walked alone toward the enemy, his long-barreled gun loaded with four bullets. As the Iroquois began to aim their bows at him, he raised his weapon and fired.

His bullets struck three enemy chieftains standing close together. Two fell dead at once, and the third was badly wounded. Then, one of Champlain's French marksmen posted to the side also fired his weapon, further shattering the quiet of the forest.

Terror stricken by the white men's "thunder sticks," the Indians fled in wild panic.

Champlain and his allies had triumphed. But never would the Iroquois forget what they called the "treachery" of the French. They pledged a struggle to the death against France, and in later years sided with invading British forces.

For a time, though, Champlain and his allies remained triumphant. Following a victory dance and

*This detail from a painting by R.L. Dowling depicts
the first battle in the French and Indian War near
the future location of Fort Ticonderoga.*

Lake Champlain

feast, he and his party marched through what is known today as Vermont and upper New York State.

On their way to the scene of battle, the French warriors had come upon a lovely lake, one that so pleased their commander that he gave it his own name. And so it remains today — Lake Champlain. It was along the southern shore of that very lake that the fateful clash with the Iroquois had taken place.

38

CHAPTER FIVE

MONTREAL

In the spring of 1610, Champlain and his Indian allies once again waged war against the Iroquois. In one bloody clash, Champlain was struck in the neck by an arrow. He pulled it out with his bare hands and continued fighting until the battle was won.

Word of Champlain's heroism spread quickly among the Indians. He became known as a man of great courage, one who never failed to defend his friends.

Shortly after his victory over the Iroquois, Champlain returned to France. There he did something truly surprising. He arranged to marry Hélène Boullé, the beautiful daughter of a wealthy royal follower. At the time, the gallant French adventurer was forty-three; his bride-to-be was twelve.

Because Hélène was so young, it was agreed that she would remain with her parents for two years before joining Samuel in Canada. It is uncertain just why Champlain chose Hélène except that she was so beautiful and that, by marrying her, he could greatly improve his shaky financial situation.

*War between Champlain and
his American Indian allies
began once again in 1610.*

In the spring of 1611, Champlain parted from his child bride and made his way to Quebec. Almost immediately he set out to explore the area where the Ottawa River joins the Saint Lawrence River — the location of present-day Montreal. There he hoped to found a major French settlement.

He immediately chose a fertile location beside the Saint Lawrence and called it Place Royale. Then, seeing a lovely, quiet island in midstream, he decided to build a fortress there. The island so appealed to Champlain that he named it Ile Sainte-Hélène, after his young wife.

Soon after beginning construction at Place Royale, Champlain left to meet with his Indian allies, the Hurons. On the first night they sat around a council fire. According to custom, everyone smoked pipes in silence for a time. Then the Indian chiefs and Champlain exchanged gifts. The Indian chiefs gave Champlain beaver skins, and Champlain gave the Indian chiefs hatchets, knives, and fishhooks.

After that, the two groups began to bargain. The Hurons finally agreed to allow a group of forty or fifty French soldiers and workers to explore their territory. Perhaps later, they said, the French could build armed settlements there to protect the Hurons against their common enemy, the Iroquois.

Champlain thus had gained many favors from the

As a token of friendship, the Hurons brought beaver skins to Place Royale. In exchange, the Indians received hatchets, knives, and fishhooks.

Hurons, probably because they trusted him. They knew he was fair and just, and they truly believed he was their friend. From his first meeting with the native peoples, Champlain accepted their style of living. He did not try to force them to follow the white man's ways.

The Hurons offered to escort their white friends back to Quebec. On the way, they complimented Champlain by challenging him to shoot the Lachine Rapids with them. It was strange that for all of his experiences as a seaman, the great French commander had never learned how to swim. And the Lachine Rapids were a menacing, swirling barrier of water and jagged rocks.

To shoot the rapids in a birchbark canoe, even with experienced Hurons at the paddles, could mean death. Yet to refuse the honor of the Hurons' challenge would be to show cowardice, and thus to lose face with them forever. Champlain accepted the challenge and became the first white man ever known to have conquered the Lachine Rapids.

Champlain returned to France once again to raise money and finally persuaded the Prince of Condé, a greedy French noble, to lend his support to a new trading company. That company would grant licenses, for a price, to any traders who wanted to do business in Canada. Champlain was given command of all of the company's affairs in the New World. In effect, he was to be the ruler of New France, with the right to punish all lawbreakers.

The Habitation at Place Royale as it appears today.

Still, he had only enough money to recruit a handful of soldiers, too few of them to move ahead with the task of building a permanent fort at Place Royale (Montreal).

Instead, returning to Canada, he set out with a small band of Frenchmen and Indians, hoping to find Hudson's Bay. It might even be possible, he thought, to discover a network of rivers leading to the Pacific Ocean, the long-sought "Northwest Passage" to Asia.

But Champlain's daring journey into the wilderness failed to reach its goals. Hudson's Bay remained, at least for a time, a mystery. So, too, did the dream of an all-water route to the Pacific.

CHAPTER SIX
THE
HURONS
AND THE
IROQUOIS

Champlain spent the autumn of 1613 in Paris preparing his second book, *Les Voyages du Sieur de Champlain*. The book told of his adventures in Acadia, Quebec, and Montreal. While in Paris, he convinced several merchants to contribute money toward the recruitment of soldiers to serve in New France.

During that time, he also inspired leaders of the Catholic church to raise enough money to feed and equip four missionaries to serve among the Indians. It was his hope that they might begin the work of converting the Indians to Christianity. As he grew older, Champlain became more religious, and missionary work was increasingly important to him.

Along with service to God came service to France. On arriving in Quebec in 1615, Champlain decided that French interests could best be served by waging war against the Iroquois. Such a war would tie the Hurons closer to the French as trading partners. With victory, exploration of Canada would be easier. At the same time, French aid might well encourage Indians to

44

LES VOYAGES

DV SIEVR DE CHAMPLAIN
XAINTONGEOIS, CAPITAINE
ordinaire pour le Roy,
en la marine.

DIVISEZ EN DEVX LIVRES.
OU,

IOVRNAL TRES-FIDELE DES OBSERVA-
tions faites és descouuertures de la Nouuelle France : tant en la descri-
ptiõ des terres, costes, riuieres, ports, haures, leurs hauteürs, & plusieurs
declinassons de la guide-aymant; qu'en la creãce des peuples, leur super-
stition, façon de viure & de guerroyer: enrichi de quantité de figures.

Ensemble deux cartes geografiques: la premiere seruant à la na-
uigation, dressée selon les compas qui nordestent, sur lesquels
les mariniers nauigent: l'autre en son vray Meridien, auec ses
longitudes & latitudes : à laquelle est adiousté le voyage du
destroict qu'ont trouué les Anglois, au dessus de Labrador,
depuis le 53e. degré de latitude , iusques au 63e. en l'an 1612.
cerchans vn chemin par le Nord, pour aller à la Chine.

A PARIS,
Chez IEAN BERJON, rue S. Iean de Beauuais, au Cheual
volant, & en sa boutique au Palais, à la gallerie
des prisonniers.

M. DC. XIII.
AVEC PRIVILEGE DV ROY.

Champlain spent the fall of 1613 writing
his second book on his experiences in
Canada, Les Voyages du Sieur de Champlain.

become Christians. For Champlain, fighting a war never was an end in itself; it was the means to greater ends.

By July 26, 1615, Champlain's war party had reached Lake Nipissing, home of the friendly Nipissing Indians. A few days later, the French leader dipped his fingers into the waters of Lake Huron, the great "inland sea" he had heard about since first arriving in Canada. A young French scout and a French priest had been there before him, but it was Champlain who explored and charted the shoreline.

On August 1, Champlain reached Huronia, the home territory of the thirty thousand Huron Indians. At one native village after another the Indians happily greeted Champlain with cries of "Ho, ho, ho!"

The Hurons lived in growing fear of raids by the Iroquois. They knew that Champlain was a fierce fighter and a loyal friend to his Indian allies, one who could help them make war on the Iroquois.

Champlain knew that if he failed to stop the Iroquois raids on fur-trading routes, French business-men soon would refuse to back him with money. Everything he had worked for would be lost. War, he decided, was necessary.

Before making war, however, the Hurons insisted on a time of feasting and dancing. Day after day Champlain waited for the Indians to finish their fun and depart for battle. At last the ceremonies ended, and about five hundred Indians prepared to march — far fewer men than the Hurons had promised.

46

Before entering into war, the Hurons
would spend days feasting and
dancing in preparation for battle.

It was September 8 when the march to combat actually began. Then, along the way, the Hurons insisted on taking precious time to hunt deer and bears. They lost even more time by capturing enemy warriors and torturing them for pleasure, as was their custom.

At last they reached their goal, an Iroquois fortress on Lake Onondaga, close to the location of present-day Syracuse, New York. More importantly, the fort was well constructed. Champlain's Indian allies showed almost no sense of discipline in combat. They agreed to Champlain's plan of battle and then did as they pleased. Some tried to set fire to the log walls of the fort, but the Iroquois easily put out the flames with buckets of water.

The Hurons and Champlain's
men prepare to battle the Iroquois

Even the long-barreled guns of the Frenchmen could not turn the tide of battle. At last, the French forces and their Huron allies the withdrew in defeat.

Champlain had been struck in both legs by poisoned arrows, and he had to be carried through wind and snow, in a basket lashed to the back of a Huron warrior. On reaching Huronia, the Hurons refused to provide a canoe and escort for Champlain's return trip to Quebec. Instead, they insisted that he and all of his men spend the winter at Huronia, planning for future combat.

Champlain was ashamed that he had lost the battle. He had been embarrassed before both friendly and

48

unfriendly Indians. However, tough, strong, and courageous, he took pride in driving on where other men might have turned back. Much of his remaining life was devoted to surviving for the sole purpose of aiding in the growth of New France.

During his winter with the Hurons, Champlain came to know them well. He watched them hunt, fish, and feast. He watched them worship what he called "the Devil," to him a god of evil. He enjoyed seeing them at their games, which included lacrosse — to Champlain less a game than a form of warfare. He admired the fine, strong bodies of the men and the beauty of the women.

Yet much that Champlain saw troubled him. He knew that the Hurons prided themselves in their skillful thievery. They enjoyed slowly torturing their prisoners to death and then eating the bodies. Despite this, Champlain looked forward to the time when French and Indian people would marry each other. They would, he was sure, form a strong new race, loyal to France and also to God.

To gain his ends, Champlain worked hard to hold together the tribes most friendly to him. Once, a small quarrel between the Hurons and the Algonquins showed signs of growing into open warfare. Both tribes, however, trusted Champlain as an honest, reasonable man. They agreed to do as he suggested and to stay at peace. Gradually, Champlain came to be known by the Indians of Canada as the white man who cared most deeply about them.

Yet, try as he might, Champlain failed to win proper support from his government in France. In 1617, he pleaded with the king and his court for soldiers, settlers, and money to strengthen his beloved colony, but few in Paris were willing to listen to him. Some actually laughed at him.

In 1618, he returned to Canada with only one new settler, his own eighteen-year-old brother-in-law. Six years later, the entire French population of Quebec had grown to only fifty-one.

Meanwhile, in 1620, Champlain brought with him to the New World his beautiful young wife, Hélène, by then in her early twenties. The Indians were fascinated by her. A titled lady with elegant clothing and manners, Hélène was the center of attention at Quebec. But for her the settlement held little joy. She had nothing to do. Unlike Paris, Quebec had no shops, bustling crowds, or interesting gossip. As day followed day, she became ever more unhappy.

Champlain, meanwhile, involved himself daily in work, especially the construction of a fortress on the towering cliffs overlooking Quebec City.

At that time, Champlain began to work with some success toward better relations with the Iroquois. To him, the future looked brighter. When he sailed for France in August 1624, however, the French explorer had one great cause for sorrow. Hélène had decided to return to Paris with him and never again to come to Canada.

The strong stone buildings of Place Royale, Quebec,
as they appear today.

For four years she had survived the dreariness and boredom of Quebec. No longer a child, but a spirited twenty-five-year-old woman, she longed for the excitement of life in Paris. Champlain, fifty-six, preferred the company of his rugged French and Indian comrades and the unspoiled beauty of the Canadian wilderness. And so they parted.

CHAPTER SEVEN

FINAL VOYAGES

In 1626, Champlain returned to Canada, bringing with him six Jesuit priests. He hoped that they would succeed where earlier priests had failed in converting the Indians to Christianity.

For two years, the French settlers suffered from hard times. Then, in the summer of 1628, the very existence of Quebec City was threatened. With France and England at war, six English ships approached the city and demanded its surrender. Low on food and ammunition, Champlain still refused to give up.

Fortunately, his bluff worked. The British commander, David Kirke, proved to be more interested in furs and rich merchant ship prizes than in waiting several weeks to capture a tiny frontier city. Instead, the British turned back to the coastline to hunt for loot.

Shortly afterward, news reached Quebec that the powerful French leader, Cardinal Richelieu, had formed a new company, the "One Hundred Associates," to rule

*In 1626, Jesuit priests arrived in
Canada with the hopes of converting the
Indian peoples to Catholicism.*

all of Canada. Champlain was one of the One Hundred
Associates. Richelieu at once sent urgently needed supplies and two hundred settlers to the New World. Before
the relief ships could reach Quebec, however, David Kirke
intercepted them and seized the supplies. During the
cruel winter that followed, Champlain and his men
nearly starved. They survived mostly on eels bought from
the Indians and roots and barks found in the woods.

On July 19, 1629, three powerful warships arrived

near Quebec. They were commanded by David Kirke's younger brothers. As David Kirke had in 1628, all of the Kirke brothers demanded the city's surrender.

This time, Champlain had no choice. His men were weak from hunger. There was almost no gunpowder. No help could be expected soon from France. An armed struggle almost certainly would have ended in the death of all of the city's defenders.

The Kirkes offered safe passage for the French soldiers and settlers to England and from there to France. With deep sorrow, Champlain agreed to the terms. But he vowed that if, somehow, God would help him to return to Quebec, he would build there a mighty church.

In October 1629, the British ships carrying Champlain and the other French colonists docked at Plymouth, England. There they heard astonishing news. A peace treaty had been signed between France and England on April 29, well before Champlain's surrender of Canada. Almost certainly, therefore, Canada still belonged to France.

Champlain was overjoyed. In 1632, King Charles I of England agreed to restore Canada to France in exchange for a payment of money, much of it going to the Kirke brothers for their victory.

In May 1633, Champlain once again arrived in Canada. At Quebec, he found much of the French settlement burned to the ground by the British and the entire colony in terrible condition. Although more than sixty-five years old, he began energetically began to rebuild Quebec. To fulfill the personal promise that he made to God when he surrendered the city, he built a church to Our Lady of Recovery.

As soon as possible, Champlain met with his Indian allies. He promised them aid against the Iroquois, who once again were raiding the trade routes. Meanwhile, however, Cardinal Richelieu had lost interest in Canada. He never provided the handful of soldiers that Champlain assured him would have been enough to conquer the Iroquois warriors.

Still, the fur trade continued to grow and the French merchants to prosper. Work advanced on the fort and on storehouses for fur at Quebec. A new settlement was started at Trois Rivierès, between Quebec and the location of present-day Montreal. Settlers began to arrive in larger numbers, including wealthy nobles with land grants from the king. An explorer sent westward by Champlain returned after a year to report the discovery of Lake Michigan and Green Bay. New France was expanding.

At last completely in control of French interests in Canada, Champlain was happy. The Indians loved him as a father. The Jesuit priests had come to look upon him almost as a saint. He grew more and more religious, so that Quebec became a city of prayers and fasting. Holy books were read aloud there every day.

In October 1635, Champlain fell seriously ill. As he

A portrait from 1636 of Cardinal Richelieu

grew weaker he dictated his will, leaving much of his
wealth to the church he had built at Quebec. Devoted
French colonists gathered at his bedside. The Jesuit
priests prayed for him.

On Christmas Day 1635, Samuel de Champlain died.

The Indians brought wampum belts to the funeral in memory of their white friend. They said kind words to the French mourners.

When Hélène learned of her husband's death she entered a convent, choosing to become a nun rather than to marry again. Several years later she gave a large sum of money to found a new convent in the French town of Meaux. There she remained until the time of her death. Unhappy, childless, she had gained little from her marriage to a man whose first love was always "God and country," and whose greatest pleasure was his work in cold, forbidding Canada.

* * *

During Champlain's lifetime France took little notice of him. To most Frenchmen, Canada seemed distant and unimportant. Even well-educated Parisians denied its worth, sometimes speaking of it as a Siberia. It was only later, after the British again seized New France in warfare (1763), that the French finally realized just how wise Champlain had been.

Even then, however, the life of Champlain remained somewhat distant and remote. He lacked the glamour that leaves crowds cheering wildly. Instead, he was a quiet hero — a man of courage, character, and honor. Probably he never missed the popular applause. To him, the thrill of adventure was enough in itself.

His satisfaction came in dreaming great dreams for Canada and in working to make those dreams come true. Eventually, many of Champlain's dreams for Canada came true. He looked forward to a strong, independent country, made prosperous by its fishing, farming, timber, and trade, and today just such a Canada exists.

That the land is no longer mostly French or faithfully Catholic is not the fault of Samuel de Champlain. He gave the last thirty-two years of his often lonely life to the task of mastering a vast continent. The task was worthy of his imagination and capacity for wonder.

No other man so well deserves the title "Father of New France." Few of history's great adventurers ever lived so selflessly.

IMPORTANT DATES

c. 1567	Probable date of birth for Samuel de Champlain.
1586–1598	Champlain sides with French Catholics in bloody struggle with Protestants.
1599–1601	Visits West Indies, Mexico, Panama for King Henry IV of France.
1603	Sails to Canada with Francois Pontgravé to pursue trade with Indians and establish permanent French settlements. Writes report of his experience, later published as book.
1604	Returns to Canada with Pontgravé and founds French colony of Acadia. Many Frenchmen lose their lives during frigid winter season.
1605–1606	Visits Maine and site of present-day Boston. Spends winter on western coast of Nova Scotia.
1606–1607	Champlain establishes close contact with Micmac Indians of Acadia, working toward trade and friendship.
1608–July 3	Champlain and Pontgravé found Quebec.
1609	French side with Huron and Algonquin Indians in bitter conflict against the Iroquois. "Lake Champlain" named in honor of French commander.
1610	After victory over Iroquois, Champlain returns to France and marries twelve-year-old Hélène Boulle.
1611	Champlain builds temporary fort at site of today's Montreal. Fails in quest to find Hudson's Bay.
1613	Champlain writes second book, *Les Voyages du Sieur de Champlain*.
1615	French and Huron forces defeated by Iroquois close to site of today's Syracuse, New York.
1616–1624	Champlain tries with little success to obtain greater support from Paris for the Canadian colony.
1620	Champlain's wife joins him in Canada, but after four years decides to return to France.
1628	Although English forces demand surrender of Quebec, Champlain refuses.
1629–July 19	Champlain finally surrenders to powerful British army.
1632	King Charles I of England restores Canada to France. Champlain returns to build new settlements and to expand role of Catholic church.
1635–Dec. 25	Champlain dies. Learning of his death, Hélène chooses to become a nun.

A NOTE ON SOURCES

Champlain's writings have been collected, translated into English, and edited into six volumes by the Champlain Society of Toronto. A shorter but very fine collection of documents is W.L. Grant's *Voyages of Samuel de Champlain, 1604–1618*.

Two excellent works by earlier historians are John Fiske's New France and New England and Francis Parkman's classic *Pioneers of France in the New World, Part II: Champlain and His Associates*.

The outstanding studies by recent historians are *Champlain: The Life of Fortitude*, by Morris Bishop, and *Samuel de Champlain: Father of New France*, a truly memorable book by Samuel Eliot Morison.

Particularly useful for younger readers are:

Coulter, Tony. *Jacques Cartier, Samuel de Champlain, and the Explorers of Canada*. New York: Chelsea House Publishers, 1993.

Zadra, Dan. *Champlain: Explorer of New France*. Mankato, Minn.: Creative Education, 1988.

INDEX

ABOUT
THE
AUTHOR

William Jay Jacobs has studied history at Harvard, Yale, and Princeton and holds a doctorate from Columbia. He has held fellowships with the Ford Foundation and the National Endowment for the Humanities and served as a Fulbright Fellow in India. In addition to broad teaching experience in public and private secondary schools, he has taught at Rutgers University, at Hunter College, and at Harvard. Dr. Jacobs presently is Visiting Fellow in the Department of History at Yale.

Among his previous books for young readers are biographies of such diverse personalities as Abraham Lincoln, Eleanor Roosevelt, Edgar Allan Poe, Hannibal, Hitler, and Mother Teresa. His *America's Story* and *History of the United States* are among the nation's most widely used textbooks.

In the Franklin Watts First Book series, he is the author of *Magellan, Cortés, Pizarro, La Salle, Champlain*, and *Coronado*.